# Between Crumbs and Tears

By A'marie Ryze

Published by A'marie Ryze Press



Cover design by Brianna Sanford
Printed in the United States of America

ISBN: 979-8-218-69009-0
First Edition

For permission requests, email:
contact@amarieryze.com

To the nights I thought I wouldn't make it.
To the tears that wouldn't stop, the silence that screamed, and the strength I didn't know I had.
This book is proof that I lived through it. That I rose.
That I healed.

# What Inspired Me

I've always been a writer—
but I never had the push to pursue it.
Until a very fickle man
pushed me right off the edge.
Had he not caused such devastation in my life,
I probably wouldn't have gotten to this point.
But God has a way of making beauty from ashes.

The Spirit of the Sovereign Lord is on me, because the Lord has anointed me to proclaim good news to the poor. He has sent me to bind up the brokenhearted, to proclaim freedom for the captives and release from darkness for the prisoners, to proclaim the year of the Lord's favor and the day of vengeance of our God, to comfort all who mourn, and provide for those who grieve in Zion— to bestow on them a crown of beauty instead of ashes, the oil of joy instead of mourning, and a garment of praise instead of a spirit of despair. They will be called oaks of righteousness, a planting of the Lord for the display of His splendor."

— Isaiah 61:1–3 (NIV)

## to Write This Book?

Following my heart has endlessly led me to dead ends.
This is a full, deep dive into my journey of moving forward—
picking up the pieces and standing up after a tough fall,
even when it hurts.
It's about coming to terms with truths that are as painful as they are pragmatic and revisiting the steppingstones that shaped me into the woman I've become...and the one I've still yet to be. It took years of heartache and disappointment to arrive at this place—and I'm so proud I finally did.

# Table of Contents

# The Seeds You Sow

## Quintessence

Opening my eyes to his, so close to mine
I could feel the air flowing out of his nose.

His morning breath tart and pungent seeping through his lips.
His snores, loud like thunder rumbling down at me.
But for him,
I'd sleep beside it all and smile.

I tell myself it's a gift the way I gravitate toward and love men
who are incapable of loving anything or anyone
besides themselves.

I convince myself that it's my duty.
I'm this way for a reason.
So I sit back wide-eyed, lips in the perfect pout
and listen.

Opening my heart...
and my legs don't fall far behind.
He exchanges what I later learn is emptiness
for validation of his manhood.

A disarray of strung-together beautiful lies
each word more detrimental than the one previously spoken

He's an undiscovered poet. How can this be?
A man of such magnitude—and he's right here
on top of me.
Sweating in my eyes, droplets falling on my breasts...
We've found each other.
This may be the best chapter of my life yet.

## Chosen

I began starving myself and taking injections for him.
He never called me fat —
At least not directly.

Instead, he'd go on about the weight I was in 2018,
and how it was so much more appealing.
I was constantly reminded of the same weight
before I carried a child and became a mother.

The same weight
that couldn't keep him faithful then,
so how could it possibly now?

But I was devoted,
so, I listened.
Because beauty and love are both pain and sacrifice.
Little did I know,

This is where I would meet my demise.

## Placebo Effect

Good morning texts stopped.
Calls were constantly met with silence.
I was heavily acquainted with his voicemail.
At times there were excuses,
and others, there were not.

Chasing someone who loves the chase
and not you
will always land you in last place.

You know you're special
and that you radiate love and light,
but you stay anyway for a love that does not serve you,
when there is a love out there anticipating your arrival.

How long will it take?
How much more are you willing to break?
How long will you cry for someone
who wouldn't shed a tear for you to save your life?

# When Hearts Play a Melody

Drape me in love,
He's such a brilliant man.

Stirring up my insides
without lifting a single hand.

Breathing into me —
my pulse drops and my knees grow weak.

We slow-dance near open flames,
with bursts blooming behind our eyes.

And I think—
I don't ever want to leave this place.

Perched on the brink of blissful serenity...
just from the gazes shared between you and me.

## Residual Chaos

I wish I'd been more genuinely loving,
and embraced the time we had together.
I've lost so many of my most precious people lately,
and it got me thinking of you today.

These men don't value me,
they don't see me for who I truly am —
my love, my kindness, my loyalty, my heart, my worth.

I'm disposable,
nothing more than a glorified object
to contribute temporary pleasure while they soak up my AC
and exchange sob stories for depth.

They don't care to learn me,
seek a future or know me.
They don't care to explore me outside the four walls of my bedroom.

They don't recognize that I'm a woman,
a woman with a heart that just wants to nurture,
care, help, and cater to someone.
A woman with a soul that's seeking a mate
to build a beautiful, fulfilled life with.

They don't care that I lose sleep,
laying awake praying, worrying,
and wondering about their well-being.
They don't care that I'm a single mom,
living paycheck to paycheck,
balancing it all while part timing as
a guidance counselor for their problems.

They completely degrade me, humiliate me,
and fill me with orgasms that later expel themselves as tears.
(Sorry for that dad)

I wish I had spent more time with you,
and had your guidance to equip and shield me
from some of the displeasures of life
I'm currently dealing with.

They look me in my eyes,
piercing through me with their proclamations of love,
building a world within my mind that I later realize is actually a wall.
I'm left to break through something I was never prepared for,
so it just ends in a crippling cycle of my downfall.

## Sweetheart From the Start (Sunshine)
## for my son

I love you more than life. You're my little burst of sunshine.
The moment I heard your heartbeat; it was like we immediately aligned. From that moment on, we've always been in perfect sync.

I remember before your due date, everyone was so eager to meet you—but you and I had already formed our own special little bond. Those little kicks of yours were endless, until I'd turn over to the side you preferred. I think of your tiny little hands—or was it feet?
How you'd push them out and follow the flashlight across my belly.

So although everyone was thrilled for you to finally be born, no one knew what I was going through. Because while you were snuggled up inside me cushioned and safe, I had full control.
But I thought of once you were out...there's so many unknowns. So many things I couldn't protect you from. That very thought was enough to ruin my day sometimes knowing that kind of control was about to be taken away.

I cried over it many nights, wishing I could keep you inside me forever. But I had to be the reasonably adjusted adult that I am (and I say that loosely. hahahaha) and face the reality.
whether I liked it or not, you were coming out.
And now I'm watching you on your Xbox, fully invested in some wild little game.

Your bubbly giggles?
They're the greatest sound in my life.
I thank God for you every single day.

In so many ways, you remind me of myself.
Your personality being number one. I always thought it'd only show up in a daughter, but boy was I wrong. You're so silly and endlessly

sarcastic. I finally understand what your aunt went through with me as a kid.

Some moments with you are pure comedy and some are pure insanity. Never thought I'd be negotiating with a 4-year-old just to eat five Dino nuggets—but hey, when life gives you lemons?

One of my top tier favorite memories? You were two. I had this perfectly chilled, crisp, ice-filled water— the most divine ice-to-water ratio ever created. I'm talking "God's fridge" levels of perfection.
And you grabbed it.
Spilled it all over yourself...
and me.
We locked eyes, both of us frozen—
literally—
screaming, shivering, soaked.
Good times...
great times.

You are my bundle of joy. My unconditional love.
My sweet ray of sunshine. And the love of my life.
Your smile is the greatest part of my day. You teach me so much as we grow and learn together. And I'll teach you all I can.
Though some lessons—you'll have to learn on your own;
lessons only life can teach.

But I will be by your side, every step of the way—
whether it's rain or sunshine.
I'll love and protect you
with all of my heart.
Always.

—Love, Mommy

## Sweetheart From the Start (Sunflower)
for my daughter

Speak with me in my dreams.
I'll hold you in our special place —
where we create our inner world memories.

Our little utopia.
My sweet escape.
The perfect ending to my day.

I hope you always know,
my heart will never let you go.

Still to this day, I get teary-eyed sometimes —
you're a third of my soul
that I can't physically hold.

It tears me up inside,
but I believe we'll be reunited again one day.

So until that moment
when Mommy can kiss your face,
and look down into those bubbly eyes of yours...

Please always remember:
I love you,
My sweet baby girl.
Always.
—Love, Mommy

# Prey

The sun was so warm,
The golden rays danced across my skin,
The air tasted sweet, and the breeze was cool.

He'd just set his sights on his new fool.

## We Kissed in a Place That Doesn't Exist

I was all that you needed.
It was a pleasure sifting your worries and pains away,
Rummaging through every possibility to better your life,

Convincing myself that you'd notice me and all that I do for you,
And finally ask me to be your wife.
Surely, after 6 years, you'd be ready now.

But, you had a life outside of me
that I couldn't begin to comprehend—

A 2-year-old child and a whole girlfriend.

## Daunting Reprise

Something that's important to talk about,
but I don't like to— because of the ripple of emotions that come crashing down into me when I do—
is the initial moment when I realized and accepted that you never loved me.

How deafening that is,
the way the pain fills me like wet cement,
and I feel every morsel hardening within my chest.

It's suffocating.
It's humiliating.

It's enough to make me sit in my car and let out the most primal scream I never knew was inside of me.
But that's what you made me,
this is who I've become.

It's accurate.
It's unbearable.
It's raw,
but it's what I need in order to heal.
And for the first time in a long time,
I'm experiencing something real.

The tears, the pain, the pang of heat boiling in my chest,
flowing through my lungs, and the tightening of anxiety as
every nerve in my body rushes to my throat.
I get choked up with pouring tears in what's now very loud silence.

I'm left broken by a master crafter
who I sadly mistook as my happily ever after.

## Origins 01

By birth, I was given a mother.
But by life, I was gifted a grandmother —
a woman who, if I'm being honest, was sick and tired.
and honestly pretty fed up with this world.

All she really wanted was to sit back,
watch a good movie, and enjoy a beer or two…
or let's be real — a few.

From the moment she came into this world,
she was assigned the role of caregiver —
first to her siblings, then her parents.
Eventually she had a family of her own
And later became a nurse and carried that same
responsibility.

She supported everyone around her.
Went the extra mile.
Did what was expected of her —
and then some.

It got me thinking.
what does it feel like to be a prisoner in your own life?
Can you imagine the internal warfare?
The quiet strife?
The very thoughts that kept her awake at night?

Well… I can.
Because it's a curse that's been passed down.
Year after year. When you devote any and everything you
have to every single person around you leaving nothing for
yourself, that's not living life — it's a living lie

And waiting for the day someone saves you only manifests discontent
because they hold all the power that you should wield.
But you don't know that you're special, so you inadvertently hand
it to them, misconstruing your self-worth by banking on others to
deposit love into you.

You see…my grandmother was my world.
She was the closest thing to a loving mother
I'd ever known. She wasn't the most affectionate, but her love was
shown. It wasn't until I became an adult and gave birth to a child
of my own that I realized she had a much softer side.

It was warm. It was so kind.
It wrapped me up with love inside.
She was...proud. She saw me surviving.
Moving through life, stage after stage.
Even with my failures and heartbreaks –
just seeing me still there continuing forward,
was enough to put a smile on her face

In all honesty, becoming a mother and having a child of my own
has taught me true unconditional love in its purest,
most sacred form. The way my son loves me,
and how he's so amazed by everything I do—
From picking me flowers, to his sweet scribbles, and his heartfelt
"I love you's"

He wasn't told. He wasn't asked.
He wasn't begged or coached on what it means to show love.
He was born with this inside him and it's never faded.
Even on his worst days— Which for him are when I take his toys away,
Or when I'm working tirelessly, slaving the day away because bills
don't pause due to my mood change.
He's still always there with open arms and a heart so full of joy and
love. He's redefined what love really is.

Before my grandmother passed, she and my son became the sweetest pair —inseparable in spirit, even with generations between them there.

He still asks about her every now and then, so eager to laugh and play with his buddy again.
I tell him the truth: she's in heaven, a beautiful place, and when it's our time, we'll reunite at Heaven's gates.

## Roots From the Same Tree

My sister—she just wants what's best for me. That's probably why all we do is fight. I admire her greatly; she truly gets the most out of life. She's bold, cunning, smart, and beautiful— Yet society has her conflicted, thinking she's less valuable.

How do I convince her she's perfect in my eyes?
Not just because she's my sister, but because of who she is inside—
But again how do I convince her — when I also go through the same dilemmas myself. Feeling less than, whether it's about our weight or the way we style our hair.

We just want someone to care. Someone who through it all,
will be there, And of course I could say "Men ain't shit, a real one will come along." But how can I say that to her When I don't even believe in men anymore?

## Pride's Throne

When you said those words it gutted me
I froze in time.
It was at that very moment,
when you ripped through me, that I was forced to realize
you were never mine.

All of those years, all of those dreams
my hopes, my home, my world as I had once known
had a world of his very own.

Turns out, It was only a secret to me.
Now here I am, baring it all, broken and lonely
with a pain so jarring that it's suffocating.

Do you remember how you would call me your soulmate?
How you looked into my tear-filled eyes and reassured
me nothing was going on?
Told me stop trippen you deal with enough and there was nothing
wrong?

Tears from pain. Tears from love.
From uncertainty, and a woman's intuition.
Tears from betrayal, and most importantly, from loving you too
hard and for too long.

How do you do what you do?
Is your conscience truly out of commission
to the degree that it doesn't affect you?

You bend women,
and weaponize us to your will.
What happens the day that runs out?
Will you then be able to really feel?

## A Heart Eroded

Everything about him ended in strife,
but he was the absolute love of my life.

# The Ones I Chose

I'm not the woman I was before.
I've been torn apart.
Truth is, I don't trust myself
when it comes to romantic relationships anymore
and I don't even know where to start.

## The Labyrinth Within

In the end,
I finally understood what my grandma meant.

I sat beside her at the nursing home one evening,
venting about life while she sipped her soda, laughing.
Later that night, she paused mid-sip, looked me in the eyes,
and gave me one of her classic lectures.
She told me about what really matters in life,
and how it's not about who you choose
as your emergency contact —
life chooses for you.
And you'll know.
She told me not to let petty disagreements
destroy what's truly important.

I just smiled and said, okay, I'll think about it.
I was used to these speeches,
but God… it felt good hearing her be herself again.
It was nice.

When she passed,
I knew I had to be strong.
My son was in the nurse's station down the hall,
my mom was falling apart,
my aunts were on the way,
and my sister was on the phone.

I was relieved my grandma was at peace.
So I buried the tears inside of me.

Until I saw her in the casket.
That's when the floodgates finally broke.
But I looked over at my sister —

and saw how shattered she was too —
so I pulled myself together,
because that's what my grandma would've done, too.

# April Showers

## My Problem

No one will love him like I did.
And that's not his problem —
It's mine.

## Waterfalls

Going back to him was like muscle memory.
He was attuned to every inch of my anatomy.

I was foolish, getting caught up in a moment of pleasure.
I let him drag me down and drown me—

Like I was buried treasure.

## Never Asked for Anything "Too Much"

To hold your hand, to tell the world you're my man,
to show me off around town, to let me know you were proud and
cherished me, to help me see this was so much more than an
epiphany.

Now I'm sitting here looking stupid, staring at my notebook
filling the pages with my tears from the broken years that I gave
myself to you, but somehow, I never was able to get through.
Between loving you, pleasing you, and devoting all my time,
I carried too much; I honestly thought what was yours was also
mine—In the sense of your heart, but I couldn't manage to reach it,
And you knew it…so why did you drag me along?

You fill your family with lies, but we both know the truth.
Honestly, I'd expect nothing less from them; they're just as foolish
as you—I remember when you laughed about your brother, mom,
and sister saying I was crazy, and you actually let them think that
instead of letting them know it was you being shady.
Instead of judging my heart for being hurt, they should take a look
inside of themselves and reevaluate their own self-worth.

To defend you after what you did, to stand with you and be cool
with it— As a mother, I could never allow my son to treat women
the way that you do. Your mother should be ashamed,
And your dad too…

But it's not all on you— she didn't raise you right.
She didn't teach you or your siblings a thing about life,
And your father has no idea what it takes to be a man,
And you're just like him.
Goddamn—

I never stood a chance at a true, emotionally intelligent relationship with you. I was blinded by your symphony of lies,
I never had even an inkling of a clue. You wouldn't stay out of my life,  And I finally know why— I was the safety net for when all the other women decided to spread their wings and fly.

Your parents really should have done better, because they raised a boy that switches up more frequently than the weather.
Since 2018, I stood my ground, hoping you'd show me growth I'd never seen,

But that's what they made a cold-hearted monster walking among us day by day destroying women's hearts—
Every step of the way.

## 2am Ain't Love

You should know,
breaking my heart didn't turn my love off,
as much as I wish it did.

I've been suffering, still being in love with you,
as well as with the idea
that I could never take you back,
and could never love you the same way
I once did.

I've been grieving someone
I no longer have any connection to,
and the most isolating and crippling part is—
you're someone I realized
I never even knew..

## The Catalyst

There's was cousin of mine –
who holds a special place in my heart
He was the coolest, the realest – my safe place,
the kind of love you don't replace.

I remember the joy that filled my heart
when he'd come over to the house –
my co-conspirator in snack heists
and backyard missions.

The horse rides around the yard were a favorite –
I'd laugh and beg to go so far.
After enough laps, he'd fake a fall and claim defeat:
"The horsey broke his leg for the day!"
Then back inside to play dolls and games.

I remember once when Mom went too far –
he stood up to her, bold as a star.
"Don't lay a finger on her again,"
then off we went for candy –
my best buddy 'til the end.

I remember us out on the swing set.
I was frustrated because I couldn't swing as high as him,
so he took the time to show me how,
then sat and watched me fly.
That's a moment that always stuck with me
no matter how much time goes by.

I waited for him to come back again –
like always, my hero, my kin.
But one day, the waiting turned into ache,
because everything abruptly changed.

My shield,
had ascended past heaven's gates.

Still, I dream — in skies serene and wide — we'll catch up and swing again, side by side.

One of the last gifts he ever gave me
was a mixtape of songs he made — burned just for me.
My own personal playlist, crafted with love.
It's gotten lost somewhere along the way,
but his memory? That stays. Cemented in my soul,
it grounds me — reminding me of who I am.
in ways I'm only starting to understand

What I'd give to talk to him again
while we swing and sway in the wind.

## Diamonds

I cry for the girl who once loved blindly.
I cry for the parts of her still trying to trust herself again.
I cry for everything she's been through.
I don't harbor it — I'm just working through it.

And I don't shame myself anymore
for shedding the occasional tear,
because the love I gave was real.
No games. No hidden reasons.
I just really cared.

# Resonance

My eyes have been puffy for days.
I guess all these tears I've cried
have been detoxing the naive parts of me.

Maybe I should be grateful.
Maybe I should celebrate.

I think I'm adding this week to my calendar
as my own personal holiday.

## The Edge

I carry a love so wide,
no one else could hold it —
That's the tragedy I chose,
not the one they asked for.

An apothecary can't heal
this form of disease;
It's hard to escape,
yet it found me with ease.

## Where the Compass Broke

My struggle with men unraveled
after losing those meant to guide me —
before I ever learned what it meant to be led.

## I'd Choose You

It's my first Mother's Day without Momo.
And that realization is setting in —
I can't pick up the phone,
can't pull up and sneak her sodas and hot dogs anymore.
Can't hold my five-star concerts for her while she shakes her head,
laughing at me like I'm one hit away from a record deal that ain't
coming. And it's kinda fucking me up.

I remember as a child, hosting my unsolicited weekly concerts and
talent shows. I wonder what went through her mind
when I'd randomly flip on the lights (my spotlight)
and turn her living room into my stage. Then I'd start cartwheeling
and twirling around with her wig brush in hand (my microphone),
serenading her and the furniture with Beyoncé ballads.

I'm not as depressed as it sounds — come on, it's Mother's Day.
I'm blessed beyond compare, I'm off work, spending it playing the
xbox with my little man. But I'm only human and simply put
sometimes life hurts, no matter the day so I do have my moments —
the ones where I have to grab a pillow, and let out a good scream or
two, to get my emotions regulated.

Doesn't everyone?

*Reference: "I'd Choose You"*
The title came from one of the most wholesome moments I ever shared with my grandma. One day, I was joking around with her while she was lying in bed and asked, "If you had to choose between me and my mom, who's your favorite?" Without missing a beat, she grabbed my hand, smiled, and said, "Ohh, I'd choose you." I've never let my mom live that down. My grandma has always had my back — quick to laugh with me, quick to ride at dawn if I needed her. I miss

sneaking into her room and trying to scare her. Sometimes she'd laugh…other times, I'd catch a playful tap or two.

## Even Odds

Aside from myself and my sister,
I think my mom is my son's next favorite person.
Me and her aren't really close— I used to wish that we were,
but that's just not what it is.
I've accepted it's life and just deal with it.

I won't sit here and bash her—this isn't that kind of book.
We're just two very different people,
and when life cast a line,
one of us swam away
and the other latched on and got hooked.

My son loves her dearly, and I love that for her.
With all of her loud,
all of her inner beauty…and ugly,
and all of her charisma—
he's just so accepting of her.

Not accepting in the way that I accept what is,
but accepting in such a way;
that she's lovely to him.

He gives her a form of love that I can't provide.
I've thought about it—
and there's nothing I could've done
to change the course we're on, even in hindsight.

I love my mom.
And if she reads this—
don't start crashing out thinking that I don't.
I don't love 98% of your choices,
but you're grown.

I stopped trying to change people
and threw away the facade.
If there's change to be made,
I've learned—that's completely up to God.

## Life Cycles

My mother's ailment has always been men

She's been in a ten-year relationship
That's going absolutely nowhere.

And up until recently, I was on that same path with
six years — just short a few hairs

## Soft Skin, Sharpened Soul

Communicating with the one who hurt you
under the pretense of "getting closure"
is just a reason to stay in touch.

I used to tell myself;
"If I just had closure...
If he could explain why he did this,
what the reason was, how could he?
Or at the very least what I did wrong..."

Closure this, closure that —
I truly believed he could fix me
if he just gave me the right answer.

But that's such a problematic way of thinking.

Because how could the one who broke me
also be the one to piece me back together?

## Healing Doesn't Happen in His Bed

I was your missing piece,
but you denied and disposed of me
making your intentions clear.

I spiraled into crippling depression. My sister watched with tears in
her eyes. You should know, she despises you —
possibly more than I do.

I felt my heartbeat slow as my world turned fuzzy.
I laid there the entire night staring at the stars
until the world turned sunny.

Remember always the words you said to me —
as I always will. In reality, I was nothing more than a set of lips.
You only cared for me when you were gripping my hips.

I stood for you, and everything you loved,
kept you near my heart, and in my thoughts,
when I prayed to the good Lord above.

So convinced I could fix all your problems,
your darkness never scared me, because I knew my power.
So I took on your challenges happily.
That's where I messed up —
trying to fix problems that were never mine to begin with.

And as educated as I am,
school never prepared me for this.
So all that remained was your love stain.
I bet it all on you —
and blindly fell into the realm of your eyes.
Inhaled you deep into me and lost myself;
so convinced our relationship was a prize

Fast forward to present day, trying to discover who I am,
with you no longer being the driving force in my life.
It all has me feeling like, for the past few years —
I've been wearing a disguise.

## Mirror Mirror

I miss your confidence —
You walked around the room like you owned the bitch
When a nigga fumbles you —
Every female after is his punishment

## Homecoming

At the final moment, he put my emotional health on life support.
It was like a dam broke inside me —
tears poured more than they ever had.

I remember looking in the mirror the next day,
stunned by my own reflection.
Swollen. Eyes barely open.

I had cried so much, I couldn't make it stop.
Not just the tears — but the raw, blistering pain,
the kind that feels almost holy in how deeply it rips through you.

He'd hurt me before, but this time
was different. This time, I finally understood
what it truly meant to be brokenhearted.

And strangely, it was in that breaking
that I stopped fighting. Depleted — and for that,
I'm forever grateful.

Not to him — fuck him.

But to God. For letting the pain burn away
what needed to die. For opening my eyes to the fact
that I could survive, and love myself
the way I'd always wanted to be loved back.

That I am someone special — and I don't have to let anyone
give and take my worth whenever they decide
to toss me aside. For forcing me to love myself
more than I've ever loved a man.

This pain brought me home.

# In Full Bloom

## I Became the Storm so That I Could Survive the Flood

I've arrived at a place in my life
where I hunger for me.
Not in the sense of who I used to be,
but in the sense of; Who am I?

I've poured all of my love into those around me,
and I couldn't even compose a list of five things that define
or even excite me.

I've lost all contact with myself,
doing it all for everybody else.
And now I want to know —
Who am I?

I deserve to discover
what it feels like to be whole,
to be happy.

To just.. know,
to meet, to discover, and to fall in love
with me.

## Pulling Weeds

First of all,
Talking about your uncle does voodoo—
that explains the loyalty women have toward you.
But I've got a higher power on my side;
the protection of the Most High.

I've treated myself better than you ever did—
and I'm thankful for the hell you placed me in.
Because that fire rose miles high, as I stood there,
face to face with every lie. No more excuses this time,
there were no more corners left for the truth to hide.

I finally accepted the bullshit.
Cried. Got angry. Smiled.
Grew. Cried some more.
Used all the brokenness as brick and tears as cement
built a bridge, and walked my pretty ass right over it.

Grown ass man, asking me for money
to support your secret family.
Talking about you're in a bind,
and you're just trying to help your mama out in the meantime

But truth is...
You were doing it all for your bm, and never paid me back a single
cent. You knew I was struggling too—
but counted on me to still come through

You took advantage.
No conscience. No spine.
Just a boy in a man's body,
hiding behind lie after lie
with more excuses than time.

## Softly I Grew Thorns

I was young, foolish, and naïve.
I basically served myself up on a platter,
ready to be deceived.

So obsessed with the idea of being loved,
starving for a connection, I happily walked past
all your red flags and all it took was the tiniest bit of affection.

But that wasn't always the case —
And I've got nothing but time today.

You're the type who checks every box,
And does everything right; to make a woman feel loved.
But for you? It's all part of the scheme.

Sending three-page-long messages, professing your love,
and how God himself handcrafted me for you.

Exposing every detail of the entrails of your heart —
how it was designed for mine.
And of course, me  being me, I ate up every lie.

I was your biggest fool
Mind you —
Doing all of this, with an entire family behind my back,
playing in my face, like karma wont strike back

Bozo.

## For Delivery or Take Out

So whoever it is I get into a relationship with next,
I don't know your intentions quite yet—
However, I do know my sister wants what's best

So if you try to come between us,
I'll consider it a red flag.

Don't get too cocky or comfortable, because before you know it,
she and I will be packing you a to-go bag.

## The Quiet Undoing

I'm fairly certain
I've given in to my own pride without realizing it
under the pretense of being a homebody

When in actuality,
I've cut off all of my friends,
my phone's dry as fuck,
and I'm struggling with doubts and insecurities
that it will be like this till the end.

At one point,
for a very long time,
I prided myself on being so introverted.
It gave me peace.
It gave me a sense of security
I was my own.

But, unfortunately, as I've gotten older,
I've only grown to realize
that I'm actually just…
alone.

I find myself craving conversations and
longing for friendships.
And between solitude and bad relationships,
I've lost contact with so much.

I'm ready to step out there—
because I'm seeking a change.
But the thought of starting over
makes me just want to turn and run the other way.

## To the Girl He Cheated on Me With, the Same One He Paraded in Front of Me as If I Didn't Already Have Enough to Heal From

The very first time you called my phone, I was so confused as to what was going on I heard your voice, but I saw his name, And thought, "There's no way this nigga playing games." There's no way he'd ever cheat on me —So I let him sweet-talk, and believed it all like a dummy. The very next day, he came over to my place, and had sex, afterwards panic was written all over his face. I sat and watched his hands shake, but I chalked it up to fatigue, because he always said he was tired and exhausted from work lacking sleep and just needed some peace.

Remember when you called while I was giving my son a bath, And I told you to give me ten minutes, then hit me back? Well, as you can imagine, he didn't like that much, So he put a halt to it quick
Told me you just wanted to get into my head and fuck with it
Like the clown I was, I listened, And ignored all your calls.
And this is where the tea really started to brew, You see he painted such an unpleasant picture of you.

He told me the sob story of how you "trapped" him with a baby,
Like he didn't make a conscious decision to cum inside you.
I know. Crazy —
He went on about how the weight of the world was on him—
blah, blah. Because you were always complaining and you're "hella lazy." He never told you the truth about me— instead he just pinned us against each other, He truly had me think you were nothing more than an angry bitter son of a...
Just his baby mother—

He claimed the only thing he communicated on was on the premise of his son, but he failed to mention the parts where you two were in a whole relationship.

While you were living a whole life, I was living an entire lie.

No, he didn't disclose any of that. I stumbled upon it when he got sloppy — hiding and clinging to his phone, And of course the disappearing acts at night. The video you sent, he said it wasn't shit claiming he told you what you needed and what I was hearing and seeing not to believe it— Pleading with me stating he just wanted to see his son and cool the situation down before it got too heated

Look—the nigga cheated

He told me to change my number so that you'd "leave me alone" I bet he told you the same thing. just like in the video you sent from his phone He's a mastermind of manipulation, If it weren't for his looks I'm sure we wouldn't even be in this situation. Even though he cheats on you too— He does value you more than anybody else, This I can wholeheartedly guarantee, Whenever you'd call his phone, he'd say it's his mama or brother and take off in a heartbeat— And don't get me started on when you would reach out to me directly. He'd ghost me for months, then pop up randomly with a new sob story—his typical stunts

His breaking point was when I said fuck it— stood for myself and communicated with you. I was so curious as to why and how you kept getting my new numbers—and what was it that you wanted to say— So I answered all your questions like a woman, which he hated. Shortly after that— he professed very intensely how he loves you and that he'd send you my way if I didn't fall back. He knew that I was more of a softer woman and he took full advantage of that.

It was equally heartbreaking as it was humorous because this nigga was the one who kept hitting me back for years, Telling me how he will never leave me alone— All in my email, phone and showing up at my mama's home. Chiming in on my doorbell at 3am,
citing poetry like he's Shakespeare. "So in love"

And in the back of my mind, I was starting to have doubts.
I knew something was off, but I couldn't figure it out.

As women, We can tell when something's not adding up —
and he loved when I'd get upset, and would cut the fuck up,
I noticed that he always had you doing the same thing. He's addicted to drama—I got that nigga saved under Drama Queen.

He told me you resembled me, and that's what attracted him initially- Just like the girl in Cali, By the way — did you know he thought he fathered a child out there too? And was scared as fuck about what you would do. Basically, what I'm saying is, you're so much better than him. But it might take you some time to open your eyes and see clearly. There's no need to elaborate or dwell — I guarantee you already know exactly what I mean.

Your beautiful and you can do so much better, If you continue to ride the waves with him Be strong for yourself and your son— and with the hopes in that—he might get inspired from watching you from the sidelines and decide to get it together.

## After Everything, Me

The path to self-love
is a journey I never knew I needed.
I didn't think it was possible
to love myself—so dearly—as I do today.

If someone had told me, years ago,
that this is where I'd be,
that this is where life would lead,
I wouldn't have believed them.

Just a few days ago,
I went to the store.
I used to base my happiness
on the attention I got—
validation like currency.

But for the very first time,
it didn't faze me one bit.

I was overjoyed. Fulfilled.
And I was the sole source of it.

My happiness, my confidence, my beauty
flowed throughout me—
and it's a love I've never known.

## The Thorns Grew Sharper

I bet he thought he came up, when he said I wasn't shit—
but "a dumbass bitch".
Bet he thought he was the man when he threatened me,
Until I called his bluff... then he shut that shit up.

Mr. Spectacular.
You're so elevated.
You've got it all together—
So why the long face?

Oh, Is it because you fucked over me...
And you finally realized they'll never be another
Who can fill the presence that was my place?

I'm a diamond in the rough.
I've gone through so much—
And you get most of the credit for that.
You really know how to break us down,
Turn a woman into a clown...

But I'm good now.

I bet it made you feel real proud when you told me,
"She's the one."
Geez... she really lucked up.

And of course, I couldn't forget 'em—
So fuck your brother, sister
and your mama too.
I don't give a damn what any of them say...
I'm done with you anyway.

## Sunlight Found Me

I tried to be like him.
I figured if I turned into a shadow of the monster he was,
I'd be able to move freely like he does—

no real consequences,
no accountability,
no pain,
no sadness,
no grief.

But I couldn't fully integrate myself.
We're just not the same.

I contain a soul—
and a living consciousness.
All he contains
is a brain.

## I Know What "Hey" Means

I split myself open, and let the heartbreak pour out.
Laid in the middle of it all,
Faced every "I love you,"
Every broken promise,
And every lie dressed as forever.

I had to cry.
I had to break.
I had to cry myself to sleep.

I let go of the baggage—
That heavy chain of what I thought love should be.
I made a conscious decision
to no longer be bound by grief.

## I Kept the Crown

I was there through your chaos and calm,
holding your storms, resting with you in your quiet.
You fled every time my heart needed you near —
only to drift back into my life,
just long enough to say goodbye again.

So caught up in a psychosis of your own creation,
thinking you're irresistible —failing to realize that
a handsome face fades, and it isn't worth shit when
it's tethered to a fucked-up soul anyway.

You were the perfect lesson I wound up perfecting
in the most unexpected way.
So here's to no more stressing, no more love proclamations,
and no more schemes that involve me.

I am the dream now.
I became the light.
I became the prize.

No more longing for your affection or approval
to carry me through restless nights.

We both know I don't smoke —
but I've never been this high.
Inhaling all the freedom
and beauty life holds inside.

I'm my own palace. I'm my own escape.

20/20 vision. Thick pretty thighs.
I don't need a man to define me.
Baby, we in 2025

## Paradox of Healing

I'd wanted what every girl wants.
I'd dreamed of it since I was a child
I'd waited for it, craved it and when I thought it finally found me,
I'd already decided; This is it, he's the one.

From that moment on, everything he did I excused.
Because in my mind, this was the epic love I'd been destined for.
Drifting in his eyes, fingertips intertwined,
We shared the same heart —vibed to the same beat.
From the moment of our very first date,
he'd deeply captivated me.

Being in his arms couldn't compare
to the clarity I felt from his heart sheltering mine.
I was so sure of it all
No one could tell me otherwise —

Not even him.

I forgave,
and took more than a woman ever should.
I humiliated myself.
Sank low and smiled while doing so

I took him back, again and again,
with teary eyes and shaking hope —
begging him to choose me and just treat me right
this time.

But it never worked out.

I was in love with someone who never saw me
at the end.

The arguments,
the broken promises,
the half-love

It all finally made sense

Once I got him out of my bed.
Then my mind,
my heart,
and eventually,
my soul followed.
But it took real work.
Real tears.
Real pain.

So much fucking pain.

I'd never been so in love.
My heart had never been so touched.

And now —
it's both broken
and more healed
than it's ever been.

How exactly do I explain what I feel?

## That Girl

I was bragging to any man that came around
I was proud.
I was foolish—
I was embarrassingly mistaken.

Once upon a time,
I actually let a man convince me to hide—
like I was in witness protection or something.

Every time I pick up my old journals,
I'm baffled.
Like... he did all that
and you still didn't learn your lesson?
You still stayed?

I gave my sister hundreds of migraines.

Reading through it all,
I can still hear her voice

"You called it love – but it was the bare minimum. Think about it...
who were you hiding from? If he wanted to hide you, that should've
been all the clarification you needed – he obviously wasn't the one
Do you even bother to look in the mirror?
He had you so clouded—
but I'm here to help you see clearer.

You're beautiful.
Yeah, so what—you've gained a little weight.
You carried a child.
And people change.

You like what you like...

but let's be real—he was never a prize.
Not to mention, when you met him,
he wasn't even your type.
I'm just saying.

And you're no dummy.
That's why your journal stayed full of complaints.
Weren't y'all supposed to go on a cruise?
Ride four-wheelers together?
That beach date?

You meet his mama yet?
Did he ever really show effort?
Did you even go on one legitimate date?
I know he at least saw you on your birthday...?"

"Clarification:
The love was fake."

Once I was finally done,
she and I went to a concert to celebrate.
In the restroom mirror, I paused.

For a second—
we locked eyes, and I could hear her
speaking through my smile:

"It's about time.
We finally graduated."

## Testimony, Not a Tantrum

Every man I've ever dated—
they all have one thing in common;
I've never gone back.
No ex, no fling, no rekindling.
No conversations.
No feelings lingering.

With the exception of one.
Turns out, he's the one I really could've dodged.
Nigga was faker than knock-offs.
What a fucking fraud.

Every now and then,
I think about him.
What can I say? I'm only human.

So I pull up those screenshots and I read them back,
each line grows colder than the last —
Undeniable proof that someone I loved
saw me as nothing more than just a body to smash and pass.

And just like that,
I reset.

Snapped back into reality;
I've grown into a sharpened version of me.
Slick tongue—will slice through you with no apologies.
Still soft—but quick to cut a nigga off.

I'm not for the games.
My soul did change—but only for the better.
I nurtured and invested in me, and baby, I'm thriving.

The woman I was previously,
was a flower dying from lack of watering—
So now I pour into myself.

Working long hours—because the bills don't fade.
A blessed single mother, and I'm not complaining.
But if the bills let up, I'd be thankful for the grace.
Just saying.

Skin moisturized,
and I don't think I've ever looked this fine.
Confidence?
Shot through the roof.
You can get through devastation—
I'm living proof.

So to that bitch-ass nigga
who played games,
talked to me crazy,
and threw his baby mama—
I mean girlfriend—
in my face?

Thank you.
You're a real one.

## What I Learned in Pieces, What I Promise in Wholeness

I promise to thank God for every blessing—
the good and the painful.
Even the storms taught me something.

I promise to put myself first.
And keep myself there.

I promise to step into the sun,
to live fully,
to embrace joy without fear.

I promise to explore love—
and discover what truly fulfills me.

I promise to never let a man hide me again.
To never shrink myself for someone else's comfort.

I promise to never love so blindly
that I lose myself in the process.

I promise to cherish those who are precious to me—
and never take them for granted.

I promise to recognize red flags as warnings,
not invitations.
And to walk away the moment I see them.

I promise to never let a man isolate me
from my sister again.

I promise to protect my peace.
To honor my body,
and never let another man disrespect or distract me.

I've learned that a pretty face won't make them stay.
That nurturing them won't make them change.
And that denying my pain
won't make it disappear. I promise to always remember this

The last two relationships I've been in
were with narcissists—
And both men said they wanted their new women
to harm me.

So I ask myself:
Why am I drawn to recycled souls?

This year,
I promise to dive into that question—
with a therapist,
with truth,
with the intention to finally break the pattern.

Because I deserve freedom.
And I'm not afraid of the work it takes to get there

# Final Thoughts: Sleep Soft, Dream Big

## In conclusion, this journal-turned-book taught me so much about myself.

It helped me trace the moments that shaped me and led me to exactly where I stand today. This book has been the most transformative outlet I've ever had. It gave me space to assess, accept, and face the pain I've carried for so long—and more importantly, to begin healing and stepping into the woman I'm still becoming.

When I started writing this, I had no idea how it would end. I certainly didn't think by the end of it I'd be smiling wholeheartedly again, I honestly thought it would go on longer, but something shifted. And I owe that to three things: bleeding into these pages at all hours of the day and night, my sister... and God.

There were so many moments I looked back and thought, what a waste— what was I thinking, so much time, so much love poured into someone who never saw me, never valued me. But through writing, rereading, and pouring love into the places within me that were neglected, I uncovered something I didn't expect; something beautiful.

For years, I said I'd write my book. I'd start, then stop.
I'd get writer's block. But when this heartbreak happened…
Everything made sense. Lightening struck down into me
That relationship? It prepared me for this. My childhood? My experiences? My losses? My broken heart? It all prepared me for this— For healing. For becoming. And for everything still to come.

This book is for the women who loved too loudly, broke too quietly and are learning to love their own damn way.